Ornament of Asia

Also by Alice Kavounas:

The Invited
Open to the Weather

ALICE KAVOUNAS

Ornament of Asia

Shearsman Books
Exeter

First published in the United Kingdom in 2009 by
Shearsman Books Ltd
58 Velwell Road
Exeter EX4 4LD

www.shearsman.com

ISBN 978-1-84861-061-3

Acknowledgements:

My thanks to the editors of the following publications in which these
poems (or versions) first appeared:
Acumen Literary Magazine; Alora, La Bien Cercada (in Spanish translation);
Blinking Eye Anthology (Dec 2006); *Magma; Poetry London; London
Magazine; Poetry News; The Times Literary Supplement*; and in *Poems &
Readings for Funerals*, edited by Julia Watson, Penguin, 2004; *A Chatter of
Choughs*, edited by Professor Lucy Newlyn, jointly published by Hypatia
Trust and St Edmund Hall, Oxford, 2005; *Open to the Weather*, limited
edition chapbook by Alice Kavounas with Derrek Hines, images by
Andrew Lanyon, Cargo Press,1997.

I'm particularly grateful to Judith Kazantzis for her encouragement and
valuable suggestions over the years; Tamar Yoseloff for offering sound
advice; to Rupert Loydell, for recommending me to Shearsman; and to
my colleagues at University College Falmouth for their continued support.

Cover image from an old postcard of Smyrna (modern Izmir)
in the author's collection.

Contents

In memory of my father and mother:
Edmond Apostolos Kavounas
Mary Vergopoulou.

For Fred, in celebration of every day.

Things have different qualities, and the soul different inclinations; for nothing is simple which is presented to the soul, and the soul never presents itself simply to any object. Hence it comes that we weep and laugh at the same thing.

—*Blaise Pascal*

1660 Pensées, 'Thoughts on Mind and on Style'
translated by W. F. Trotter

Things have different qualities, and the soul different inclinations; for nothing is simple which is presented to the soul, and the soul never presents itself simply to any object. Hence it comes that we weep and laugh at the same thing.

—*Blaise Pascal*

1660 Pensées, 'Thoughts on Mind and on Style'
translated by W. F. Trotter

The Road to Ithaca

To deliver his first-born to college
he drove north to Ithaca on icy roads
facing down the one-eyed beams of snow-plows
in our big-toothed, second-hand Buick
that leaked oil, forcing us to stop
every half-hour to top up—
in bitter, wind-chill-factor weather.

Born and raised just south of Troy, amidst
Mediterranean breezes and donkeys,
my Ottoman Greek father's annual trip
must have reminded him of other journeys,
other herculean tasks he'd tackled.
But he was no Trojan warrior, no Greek
hero, just a man trying to hold his own

in America, where no one interferes—
not even when your car lets you down.
Oncoming drivers are as snow-blind as you!
My father's odyssey was repeated
every year, until my brother's graduation.
Now Ithaca has become my metaphor:
breaking down in winter, then journeying on.

This is the Gift My Mother Gave Me

"Act as if a thousand eyes are upon you"
was my mother's parting shot
every day as I left the house for school.

So I divided those thousand eyes by two—
five hundred people seemed slightly less
intimidating—and guessed that of those
five hundred, at least fifty were far too tired
to notice me. Another fifty
had, I hoped, forgotten their glasses,

and perhaps another fifty were blinded
by worry—about losing their jobs, or
forgetting to lock the door. But that still left
three-hundred fifty, all out there, waiting
for me to put a foot wrong. I figured
that a hundred of them were foreign
and didn't understand my mother's dictum.

Which still left two hundred and fifty
eagle-eyed pedestrians peering at me.
I wrote off another fifty by deciding
they were newly-weds, and so in love
they had eyes only for each other.

The last two hundred remained a problem.
I silently assigned them a book to read—
and those in a rush, the newspaper.
On the subway no one glanced at me. See?

Mother was wrong, though I tended to sit up straight, and tried not to snap my chewing gum.

On Seeing the Statue of Liberty
for the Second Time

As the tallest girl, I got to play the Statue of Liberty.
On the night, I walked on stage, raised one arm
and stood stock still, crowned, in my sickly green
costume which the teacher called 'verdigris',
our old living room curtains actually,
which my mother had sewn and draped just so.
I was proud to be the famous Statue
to hold high the familiar torch—
a flashlight concealed in cardboard.
But after an hour of holding it
straight-elbowed, well above my head
that paper cone had turned to lead.

So when it came round for me to recite:
'Give me your tired, your poor, your huddled . . .'
I, too, was *yearning*, (a verb I'd just learned),
to be free. At last, I understood the words
which I'd rehearsed. Now I sympathised with
those poor folks who'd entered New York harbour;
who, on seeing the Statue of Liberty,
were about to shed whatever burdens
they'd shouldered in their homeland.
And after their arduous sea journey,
were they ever on the brink of giving up?
Suddenly my co-star, playing Uncle Sam,
broke my train of thought, grabbing me boldly
by the (other) hand to take our bows.

Foreign-looking in that crowd, whispering
in their embarrassing language,
and applauding with the rest, were Mom and Dad.
I smiled, welcoming them to my country.

One Bedroom Apartment

From our grey concrete balcony, I watched
the huge red disc of a sun as it set—
pinned atop the Empire State, stopping
then slipping behind the skyscrapers—
a cinematic view from our one-bedroom apartment
across the East River in Queens.

We tried every combination. Mother and father,
mother and daughter, father and son, sister
and brother—we slept every which way.
Moving ourselves back and forth
from foyer to living room, to the bedroom
and back again, was just like moving furniture.

And that one bedroom, divided:
pink sheets strung along a make-shift pole
prone to collapsing in the middle of the night . . .
My goal? To grow up. Escape.

Mother's black, three-quarter grand piano
was the only stable thing in the place.
Too heavy, thank God, to shift; the centrepiece
we all played under, on and around.

I can still hear her saying—*Again, please,*
as she taught yet another reluctant child
'The Spinning Song', accompanied by
the din of neighbours' broomsticks from below.

The Red Sofa

(A 12-piece suite)

I

A child napping in the afternoon. She is four, perhaps five years old. It's long before the days of sending children to school as soon as they can talk.

Her mother is making the beds, or sitting at the piano, or stirring something in the kitchen. The sun crosses the living room, warming the sleeping child on the velvet sofa. They live six floors up in a small, rented apartment with a view across Queens to the Empire State Building, and the radio is permanently tuned to the classical music station, WQXR.

Her brother is older, and at school.

At eight o'clock each evening their father returns from the office. The children have already eaten; their mother would join them only if her husband were planning to work unusually late. Before supper, their mother reads to them from the Bible for exactly fifteen minutes. She has begun from the very beginning. By the time the little girl is twelve, they will have reached the New Testament.

Peter Pan Diner

Cute cousin Nick—flirting at the till
instead of studying—how my brother and I
envied him and his part-time job. It gets better.
Straight out of high school, cousin Nick
goes and marries his childhood sweetheart
proposing over a cream soda
as he perched on leatherette and she waitressed
in my uncle's all-American (Greek) diner,
where a nickel played you Elvis's latest.

Meanwhile, my brother and I continued
our adolescent journey, book-led,
taking exams, earning qualifications,
visiting the old diner less and less.
Cousin Nick, a local hero now,
was running dealerships, becoming big
in small real estate; moving further
to the right. We were losing touch.

Our aunt and uncle, still working non-stop,
still drinking coffee with the regulars,
listening to their stories, still chain-smoking . . .
We heard that at eighty-two, they divorced;
he lived on 'til ninety-four, she 'til ninety-eight.

Peter Pan lives on, jacked up, trucked
to another state and renamed Betsy's.
Still a teenage hang-out, but with a new jukebox
and fresh leatherette, should you care to propose.
If you stop there, play a song for me.

Aivali

This neck of sea
swift running
is where you crossed
to escape a death
more certain than
the heat of the mid-day
sun as it beats down
on this stretch of beach
where I stand and peer
at the coast opposite
searching for a sign
an indication of some sort
the flicker of an oar
a tell-tale rhythmic plash
of a prow cutting through
these Aegean straits
a sign to let me know
that somehow you sense
my presence decades later
as I grasp, at last,
what you had to go through
that night to flee
with your brothers
from Aivali
to reach this shore
with nothing left
but your lives
held onto as tightly
as the oars

in your clenched fists.
The necklace of lights
opposite in Ayvalik
comes on
yet what I see
is your Aivali. I recall
every sweet memory of it
you still held—
how your eyes would shine
as, time and again,
you'd describe to me
your long-vanished life:
Mother, father, brothers
and your band of friends—
young men playing mandolins,
making music on a Sunday
in your family's orchards of
quince, fig, peach
and plum . . . all ripe
for the gathering.

Note:
'Aivali', the Greek name for this Anatolian harbour town was changed to
the Turkish 'Ayvalik,' after the so-called 'population exchange' in 1922.

Fall Weekends – I

You were hellbent on burning the brilliant
freshly-fallen ones, mingling with
the crumpled millions that must have dropped
for years before you'd set foot here
decomposing into a thick humus
more akin to earth than leaf; slow to flare up.

How could I have known that you were elsewhere
on those crisp weekends, raking up the past,
feeding insatiable fires—from Anatolia
to the tip of Long Island. You stood there,
transplanted, like a sturdy tree yourself;
I never thought to ask
what you could see as you stirred the embers.

Fall Weekends—II

Before you was a pyramid of fire
burning day and night. As we'd go off
to play, you'd stay put, raking over
that same ground year after year,
clearing layer on layer of detritus
alone, with just the birds for company.
And, of course, your trees.
Was there a memory of another fire
rising through those leaves; your beloved
Smyrna ablaze, burning before your eyes?
You seemed content—or was it resigned—
to clear the plot of land that belonged to you,
while contemplating your narrow escape.

Before me burns this image: you, amidst
your tall North American trees, tending
that unending pyre of fallen leaves,
the fire speaking to a fire inside you.
That much I know.

Everything Is Before You

Before you is your city, burning to the ground.
Before you stands a friend who'll never be found.

Before you, the farm you were born and raised on.
Before you, the orchards, their fruit long-since gone.

Before you, your mother. She will fall to the knife.
Before you, a rowboat that will save your life.

Before you, your brothers, each wielding an oar.
Before you, safe harbour on the opposite shore.

Before you, the woman whose hand you take.
Before you are woods to clear, and cultivate.

Before you, a catalogue of mutual slaughter;
the birth of a son, then a daughter.

Before me, the earth that conceals the truth.
Before me, a portrait, the vestige of your youth.

Ornament of Asia

What if, on a day in mid-September,
I awoke as usual to this idyllic view—
a crescent of a bay—but instead of Coverack
it's my father's city, Smyrna, nineteen twenty-two,
her harbour thick with battleships flying flags
from the world's so-called fair-minded countries.

Would I sense the danger on that brisk wind?
Would I try to leave? And if I panicked
what, besides the children, should I grab?
Would I abandon everything—even
the carefully tended fig, coming into fruit.
Would I be swayed by wild rumours ...

mounted men are heading toward the city
set to sack and burn it ... Or would I chance it
and stay, thinking, we've made our lives here
for thousands of years, trading in and out
of this city. *Flee? Flee to where? How?*
Look at the ships. They must be here to save us,
I would have thought. *Would I have thought that?*

And like as not, I might have rushed the children
through the stumbling crowds, fled from the 'safety'
of our house. I'd have joined the floods of people
edging toward the harbour, that numbed procession
with no exit plan, pushing for a place
on the last steamer, to get themselves out,
to go anywhere. Anywhere but here.

What if we plunged into the sea and swam
toward those smartly dressed crews—French, Italian,
British, American—on board, standing watch—

surely they'll see us coming! We're swimming
for our lives, stroking the water like it's the last thing
we will love . . . But wait—some crews are throwing back
the swimmers like small fish . . . we see them drowning,
drowning within inches of those foreign hulls.

We dog-paddle back to shore, breathless, trapped
between fire and the sea. The ships' masters declare neutrality.
Who would have us now, orphans of the 20th century:
Armenians . . . Jews . . . Ottoman Greeks . . . Palestinians . . .
exiled on the wrong side of history.

Note:
In 1922, from the 11th–14th September, Smyrna was virtually destroyed by
fire. This was the culmination of the ongoing, brutal conflict between the
Anatolian Greeks and Kemal Attaturk's victorious army. Strabo, writing
in the Augustan age, described Smyrna as the finest city in Asia, famous
for its harbour, and as Homer's birthplace. Known as the Ornament of
Asia, Smyrna rivalled ancient Ephesus.

The Red Sofa

II

Their mother is diligent. She skips nothing, not even Deuteronomy, although none of it is very clear to any of them. There are scores of names, and puzzling events occurring in mysterious places.

For a long time, the children can grasp only the rhythm of the remote language. It soon becomes as ingrained as the classical music they hear their mother playing, and the music on the radio.

These two languages, musical and Biblical, eventually interlace, imparting to the children a vast sense of complicated and immensely beautiful sadness.

That the world is a bewildering place, becomes a familiar notion.

The native Greek accent of both mother and father is stubborn. They continue to converse in Greek. Luckily for the little girl, her older brother has taught her English from the start, and they speak to each other only in this language.

Both children are always at the top of the class. Their parents will soon come to expect this. Throughout their school years they know they must perform brilliantly.

Canary on the F-Train

'My shaggy ally'—Emily Dickinson's father
gave her a dog that became her constant companion.
Mine? A canary, and even though birds fly,
this one boarded the subway, perched on my lap
in its shiny cage, box-fresh from Macy's Pet Department.

Dumbstruck with fear, its song stuck in its yellow throat.
It was, however, under guarantee. All winter he didn't sing
a note, yet grew in strength. But it was more than enough
for me to watch him hop, back and forth, swivel
like a dancer, never miss a beat;

more than enough to mirror the twitch and tilt
of his yellow head; peer at the expert way his tiny beak
shucked each seed to gain the kernel within.
On the F-train going home, balancing that longed-for
treasure on my lap, my father had turned to me:

'Little birds . . .'—here it comes, I thought,
useful tips on the care and feeding of young canaries—
'. . . don't live for very long. Yours is no different.'
I nodded quickly to show I'd understood—
hoped the subway clatter would drown him out.

'However much you love it, one day soon your pet
will die. That's why we didn't want to buy it.' I was
too stunned to ask what 'soon' meant; his subway talk
had silenced me for weeks. I'll never know how hard it was
for him to drum this truth into his eight-year-old.

Come summer my canary travelled to the country
alongside me in the back seat, safe in his cage—
the entire length of Grand Central Parkway, Northern State,
along the Smithtown bypass—every bump and turn
a fresh worry. But canaries don't get car sick.

Once there, I brought the stand outside and stood
eye to eye with my canary in full sun. All around us
birds were singing. Suddenly, a single note!
Clear. Strong. Followed by another. It was as if
I saw the song itself rise from that yellow throat.

His singing accompanied me through childhood.
When, five years later, my canary sang its last,
my father's 'I told you so, I told you so', cut deep.
His bleak refrain still runs in counterpoint
to my canary's yellow-throated song.

Woman with a Fringe

Each week they wash, comb and centre-part
her moon grey hair. The dyeing years are behind her—
why hide your age in here? Fine and sparse,
her hair floats among the pillows, holding
by the roots to what life is left.
These past few months, it's been trimmed into
a bob. Mother, fashionable to the end . . .

But look—this week they've given her
a fringe! Madcap, I mutter to myself,
mad cap. Did she ask for any of this?

She smiles her patient smile as I approach
her chair, which she's too frail to roll forward.
My own Mother, crowned by utter strangers.

Mal de Tête

I walk around my house like a visitor,
stiff-necked, balancing my head with each step.
Tilt it one degree and my brains might spill out.
How would I retrieve those worm-like bits.
No one could knit them back together.
Who would I be then, and who am I now?

I walk around my house like someone
who once lived here not all that long ago
but left suddenly, without explanation
and feels glad to be back, to idly recall this
and that, a plumped cushion placed just so,
my dog's lead hanging on the correct hook.

I walk around the house without purpose,
recalling a visit to a space that was vast,
yet narrow, dark, cluttered with people
whose conversations kept repeating phrases
in an endless loop, syncopating with pain,
penetrating the night, resolving nothing.

What has silenced them all? The furniture
greets the air in a wordless exchange. The dog
sighs, changes position. I venture outside.
The newly-minted leaves might hold clues.

The Red Sofa

III

At sixteen the girl's brother will fall ill on the morning of an important examination, missing his only chance to compete for a scholarship.

He suffers a kind of nervous breakdown, although this particular phrase is never mentioned. The boy quickly recovers and will continue his scholastic career without further interruption.

The girl is, by now, ten.

She has begun to experience intense, recurring migraines which will continue unabated for twenty-five years, and beyond that will occur only sporadically, once or twice a year, but in a punishing series of clusters, as if to remind her of her past.

These episodes will require the very newest drugs, as well as the oldest, simplest treatments, such as lying for days in darkened rooms, whether at home, in hotels, or at luckless friends' houses, with ice cold compresses, often a bag of frozen peas, pressed against her forehead.

In the Pink

Flesh-pink cherry blossoms hang in clusters
off slender limbs, in a shimmering gold foil sky
as I lie here in this Harley Street treatment room
staring at a Japanese lacquered screen.

I am eye to eye with the setting sun.
My body's like a general's map,
bristling with pins: each tiny stab marks
a key interstice—
the fat of my palm, the crook of my knee—

and so on, in a silent room
where, hour after hour, behind drawn blinds,
each patient, suffering from this or that complaint,
contemplates, like me, another country,
inhabiting, temporarily, a more placid landscape.

Anyway, just as I start to relax,
I detect among the cherry blossoms
a scattering of crimson blots—rogue red
chrysanthemums—each fiery flower
spreading its thread-petalled bloom
unhealthily amidst the tranquil pinks.

And then, from these rogue red blooms, unwelcome
images steal across the lacquered screen.

The room feels sucked of air—stifling—
as if someone's just dialled up the thermostat to hospital-hot . . .

red/amber/red flashes me down at midnight—
police cars in lay-bys start ambushing drivers
for random checks—they're pulling me over—
you, *yes you!*

Now airport security
seizes my luggage—they're undoing all
my carefully packed bags, spilling the contents.
What is this? What exactly do you want?

What have I done?—Flushed faces appearing
from nowhere, from now on, at every window.

Flags

We walked south on 6th, against the traffic,
toward a column of sky, brand new, blank and blue—
a vacuum—funnelling us all the way downtown.
We stopped at the lights—a well-dressed woman
throwing up into a wire bin—the lights changed.

The next day, I would go to an exhibition,
see Gauguin's woodcut, *Mahna no Varva Ino*—
and think back to that woman
punctuating our journey toward what
will always be known now as Ground Zero:
once just a coda to these unremarkable streets
where my mother filed away her final years;
and where (all those decades ago) father earned our keep
travelling here by subway, in starched white shirt,
suit and tie, braving the drenching summer heat.

The makeshift kiosks were busy selling tat—
baseball-style FDNY hats; postcards
of then and now; framed photos of destruction;
homely items to pin to the railings that ring the cemetery.

There, opposite: the infamous plot,
vast enough to have housed a civilisation.
We joined the slowly moving crowd
and walked silently round and round . . .
What could I leave here—a sandal, a ring?

I saw children's indigo handprints
on a giant canvas; the hieroglyphs

of a thousand signatures; news clippings
honouring a son or daughter—the ink

already fading—heroes and heroines
in their hometown papers; banners from schools;
a love letter to a lost husband.

And, like pilgrims who offered up their rags
at ancient wells for St Audrey to heal their ills,
people in their thousands had draped their T-shirts—
torn, rain-soaked—flags flapping in the hot wind.

Note:
Mahno no Varva Ino—Day of the Evil Spirit

The Red Sofa

IV

Every evening, each child takes turns to practice the piano for precisely one hour. Their mother supervises their progress, her perfect pitch detecting a wrongly played note, even within a complex chord, from any room in the small apartment.

Their mother teaches them for the first six years, and when they each turn twelve their instruction is taken over by a Mrs Rose from the prestigious Juilliard School of Music. She's plump and friendly. Lessons are at her home, an apartment only slightly larger than theirs, and Mr Rose always arrives toward the end of the girl's lesson. He busies himself until the hour ends.

Mr Rose plays jazz and the girl longs to hear him but is too embarrassed to ask. Or even to ask Mrs Rose to ask. The couple laugh together and have no children.

Neither the girl nor her brother is brilliant at piano, and at sixteen they will stop taking lessons. Their mother, an accomplished pianist whose debut concert in Athens was at age nine, attempts to prevent this from happening.

She informs Mrs Rose that she will try everything.

Moonlit Ballroom in Corfu

for Jessica

Whoever walks out into these star-filled nights
is a poet, fluent in the language
of wave gathering, of sea against stone,
the seductive smile of a white-pebbled cove.

Whoever walks out into this September night
could, without a single lesson, name
these ancient trees whose pliant branches speak
of a now-forgotten peace.
                                            Walk with me
into the olive grove: as if in a moonlit ballroom,
sturdy dancers stand poised to unfold their swathes
of jet black tulle—local harvest beauties
preparing to offer their fruit—
their limbs moving to the island's sea winds.

How they toss and shake their upswept hair
and look—olive green eyes everywhere—
with all they possess held in readiness.

After 'The Minotaur'

The steps down to the labyrinth
narrow, steep
light up as each innocent
descends. The ladder lights up
immediately as their descent begins
so of course the ladder was there
all the time, it's there all the time
but it takes the touch
of human flesh, hands on
on the topmost rung to make it
light up. And once lit it stays lit
marking the descent
of the innocents, one by one
and we cannot help but see
the full extent see the extent of it
one steep journey made of individual steps
innocents descending individually
one rung at a time
each with his or her back to us
(you cannot descend a narrow ladder
while facing the audience)
so we can see only the back
of each innocent as he or she
descends, a journey by its nature
self-effacing, and we, the audience, know
as he knows, as she knows
there is no turning back.
Yes, there is twisting and looking over
a shoulder, yes, even looking up briefly,

pointlessly looking up, pointlessly,
but no turning back from what waits
at the foot of the ladder.

Villa Gallini

for Jessica

Yoghurt and honey
        beneath Hockney-blue skies.
The onslaught of sun
        stunning Northern eyes.
Cavafy and coffee
        Sudoku and tea.
Swimmers snaking
        down paths to the sea.
Octopus, squid
        and a dribble of peach.
Water-colour mountains
        stretching beyond reach.
Lemon-winged butterflies
        tree frogs that bleep.
Olive branches offering
        sun-dappled sleep.
Pitchers of rosé
        a melon-moon rising.
Sailboats vanishing
        behind emerald spires.
Crickets and crocs
        talk, small and deep.
Citronella candles
        guarding our feet.
Stray cats in moonlight
        swallows in full flight
            zig-zagging through
        the Ionian night.

The Red Sofa

V

The mother allows her son to put aside Beethoven's lengthy 'Moonlight Sonata' in favour of a piece of sheet music the boy bought with his pocket money. 'Davy Crocket'.

She instructs Mrs Rose to proceed with it.

This experiment with a popular tune is a brief flirtation, however, which merely prolongs the boy's lessons for a few uneasy weeks and underlines his mother's keen disappointment. He never plays the piano again.

Four years later, the girl, having mastered Beethoven's 'Pathétique', simply stops. Learning to play jazz, or turning to the violin, appeals to her. But she knows that nothing would ever be considered an appropriate substitute for the piano, and so never discusses these options with Mrs Rose, nor with her mother.

Meanwhile, the mother consoles herself with the knowledge that both children excel at school.

Their father seems entirely unmoved by these musical events.

He is proud of his wife's extraordinary talent, but has never touched the keys of their immense black piano himself. Nor has he selected a record from his wife's modest collection, placed it on the gramophone, and settled into the sofa to listen. At least not to anyone's knowledge.

Once in a Blue Moon

Suicides off Golden Gate Bridge
don't occur once in a blue moon. Blue moons
are rare, suicides are not, especially on nights
when the moon is full. Stand here with me.
Before you is the Pacific, the light
of a full moon raking wave after wave
and revealing each steel hawser
stretched as tightly as the bands of pain
drawn across your forehead. The passing cars
see nothing but a lone figure taking in
the night air—star-gazing perhaps—and if
someone saw you about to take your own
life, would they slow down; more to the point, stop?
Once in a blue moon, maybe.

Paperweights

Sunday, Feb 16th, 1941:
In the wild grey water after last week's turmoil.

A few weeks after she entered those words
Virginia Woolf walked out one afternoon
into that terrible water, toward no island
no distant shore, river-walking, offering herself
up to the elements. Standing knee-deep,
unable to go deeper, she slipped into the shallows
of the Ouse, words and all, weighed
down, weighed down, lying prone in the stone-filled
grave of her, without a splash to toll her death.

This was no accident. Before setting off
she'd left a letter, carefully composed.
As I walk along the beach, I imagine her
stopping and bending, bending and pocketing,
bending and pocketing . . . or had she been hoarding
those lethal stones all along? Had she dared,
even, to place them, just so, on her desk?
And had anyone asked, *paperweights,*
she might have whispered. *Paperweights.*

Where the Blue Air Sings

We walk east, then south in this sweaty, old shoe of a city
and head for the *faux* French café. We arrange ourselves
on the black metal seats, slick from the tail-end
of hurricane Frances. Jackhammer drills
puncture conversation. Tinted windows
soar above us, dwarfing the office crowd—
all noshing and sipping at this urban
watering hole, blooming with yellow umbrellas.

We board the jitney and ride out to where
the ocean's roar and swell will welcome us—
miles of forgiving sand covering
and uncovering our tracks—where the blue air sings . . .

A chorus of crickets kick-starts the night, their rusty ditty
lulling us to sleep. The milk train's distant whistle
answers the wood owl's hoot 'n giggle . . .
the salt-laden sea burnishes the flesh, returning us to ourselves.

Waiting for the Fireworks in Falls Village

i.m. Sara Ann Freed

We five surviving friends of a friend
find ourselves on a grand porch, enveloped
in darkness, invisible to each other.
An immense valley faces us, with nothing
between us and the Berkshires but trees.
Mosquitoes carrying Nile Fever,
inquisitive bears—no one dares turn on lights.

A storm is definitely approaching—listen!
Is that a crack of thunder—we need rain,
or have the fireworks at last begun?
And that shower of tiny lights? Oh, just clusters
of lightening bugs, animating the night.

As we wait for the sky to be punctured
by a raucous performance of rockets and flares—
July's annual brilliance—we reminisce
about childhood summers; how the decades
vanish; about our friend.

The fireworks must be elsewhere
this year. Let's meet in the garden at midnight.

Self-consciously, we form a perfect circle—
someone strikes a match—and, slowly at first,
we make contact—each touching the tip
of one fiercely lit sparkler to another,
and another, and another . . . holding

our own small ceremony of light, as if
to make absolutely sure that from somewhere
in this vast ether, our friend who joins us
can gaze at us, standing here as one, ablaze.

The Red Sofa

VI

One winter evening, the family travels into Manhattan to hear the mother play the piano accompaniment for a classical singer who is performing at the Carnegie Recital Hall.

Although they own a rather fine car, a grey, solemn, second-hand Oldsmobile, they find themselves taking the subway.

As soon as they descend into the familiar, cindery, fluorescent gloom of the underground, the girl is struck by the wild incongruity, in that setting, of her mother's glamorous evening gown: a full-length, peacock green taffeta which her mother has to grab hold of with both hands in a great bunch to prevent it from blackening with soot.

The girl longs to escape. But she stays close, and the four of them, like a flock of peculiar migrant birds who follow a prescribed, if demanding route, alight and perch, one by one, on the steps of the down escalator.

Her mother continues to hold the billowing folds of her evening gown, now with one hand, the other firmly on the rubber banister to steady herself, in case the hem catches in the fast-moving mechanism, and plunges her headlong to her death.

Lunch in Ayvalik Harbour, Anatolia

Frankly, we chose the one that looked expensive,
figuring the waiters would be polite,

older—speak more than restaurant English.
They might even know Greek. I could ask

about the past, show them the photograph.
It was just an outside chance, but still . . .

The linen is pink. Impeccable.
Silently, they bring bread, water, olives,

plate after plate of *meze* as we watch
boys slither and splash in the harbour—

diving, but not for coins, just larking about.
They look like brothers, cousins. I can't help

studying their faces for a trace of my father,
his brothers. My brother, me.

The couple at the next table toss bits of bread
into the sea—minnows arrow toward each morsel

like metal shards to a magnet. Our octopus arrives,
glistening in the local olive oil, tentacles diced bite-size.

Jalem . . . Sinbad . . . Jalem . . . Sinbad . . . small boats
moored inches from our table, rock gently,

cradling young fishermen who sit mending
tangled nets. When we've eaten our fill,

we begin to stroll along the front. The boys
have gone. I give the place a backward glance.

The waiters are attacking their own late lunch.
I've come this far, yet asked them nothing.

La Sarrasine

for Linda

Flowerless oleanders, an olive tree
unpruned, a brave geranium or two—La Sarrasine
left to you, suddenly, in mid-winter.

How the details of death have absorbed you . . . tired
from arranging food and flowers for the mourners
you stand, like this house, rudderless, in the teeth of the Mistral.

At last, you allow yourself a moment,
here in the garden, to breathe. Bracing yourself,
you invite me to follow your gaze . . . Together

we stare out across the vineyards—that vast
and familiar valley of carefully tended vines,
row, upon row, upon row, shorn of fruit,

each clipped close to its roots—and then beyond
to the seasonless backdrop of pine-dark mountains
where, come the Spring, you plan to return

to scatter your father's ashes. There, you explain,
there they will join your *belle-mère's*,
which you scattered only last Spring.

Last night . . .

the banging of the neighbour's shutter
rattled through room after room after room . . . *who
will come after us? And then*

who? And then? This cold
country, warmed by a hot sun,
now holds you.

★ ★ ★

Sunday. The giant *cloche* tilts sharply
calling the faithful to church. The flowers
you left by the altar have already begun to fade.

Go quickly—single out the bright ones—
fill a jug with water,
arrange them as best you can.

Now walk carefully up the stairs
and place them next to
what was your parents' bed.

The Red Sofa

VII

The up escalator, running opposite them, is lined with grey or navy-suited men returning home from work. The girl acknowledges their stares; this is what it's like when a movie star mixes with ordinary people. She pretends not to be embarrassed, neither for herself nor for her mother.

The concert hall is full. Seats have been reserved for them near the front, on the left side so that they can see their mother's hands on the keys. The piano music and the singer begin.

Within minutes the father is seized by a fit of coughing which forces him to rush from his seat and steal up the aisle toward the exit sign. Eventually, having missed most of the concert, he returns and sits quietly.

The mother, as usual, plays fluently. Later, they all go next door to The Russian Tea Room and order expensive French desserts.

Neither the girl nor her brother breathes a word of the incident, but it's clear that their mother already knows who it was who ran up the aisle coughing. She doesn't seem angry.

They have an excitingly late night, returning in the empty subway carriage to Queens.

At the Stone Masons' Yard

Delicate trails of crushed invertebrates,
waves of weather, eddies of air and water,
miniature whirlwinds; incidents. I'm following
a storyline hard to decipher,
written in a language never spoken,
incised in majestic slabs of sediment
hidden beneath the sea or behind
a cliff face, offered up for sale to embellish

my kitchen counter; to fashion a round table.
I walk among the silent world of cloud greys,
kashmiri whites, blue pearls, nero absolutes.
A sudden shaft of sun slants across the yard
backlighting a length of pink marble,
tender and luminous, from here, as flesh.

The Red Sofa

VIII

Against both her parents' wishes, the girl goes away to college, instead of living at home and commuting by subway to an equally good college in Manhattan.

Four years later, she graduates, and again, against her parents' wishes, she moves even further away to London.

Fast forward a few years, and, much to her parents' delight, she has returned, if not to her parental home, at least to America, and settles into her first Manhattan apartment.

She is given the midnight blue velvet sofa that she used to take naps on as a child.

Her mother longed to get rid of it, and has since bought a modern one in a style called Scandinavian, defined by its pencil-thin wooden arms, and flat, tight cushions.

Wistman's Wood, Dartmoor

At last, we reach the twisted oaks
the moor's oasis in a sea of wind
while in the distance, a river zigs and zags
running like a child—thoughtlessly, with grace.
We sprawl among green boulders, lichen furniture,
and spend the afternoon discussing silence.

Pastoral Scene (After Samuel Palmer)

The harvest moon rises in blood
over the shorn fields. The golden sheaves
stand like ancient stoneworks.
Winter lies ahead. These endless fields
of stubble are hard on children
without good shoes to their name
without someone to carry them through.

Equinox

Sheaves of wheat mechanically embraced
in field after field, then meticulously sealed
in bin-bag black, scraps catching at hedgerows
all winter—remnants of another harvest.

Late March. These same fields lie cased
in silver—not with an overnight dusting of snow,
nor from the sparkle of a late frost, slow
to burn off, but thanks to the farmers' Spring ritual:

their sheathing of freshly-tilled earth against
the vicissitudes of wind and weather. How fiercely
the sun glistens on row after row; how perfectly
a hard rain dances, penetrating just so.

How plastic announces each equinox
more loudly than the dawn chorus.

Letter to a Garden

You are time well spent, making a frond-like
fist of every kind of weather, drawing water
up through your throaty tap root—
sharing it—giving permission for native
bulbs, unruly weeds, plant hunters' seeds,
to germinate into this poet's palette:
Calla Lily white, bruised reds, forget-me-not
blues, Mexican yellow, Himalayan pink,
seven shades of green.
With the wind hard at your back,
you shelter the less hardy of us:
winter jasmine, the lenten rose, peonies.

Listen to the birds in your hair!
Another spring. You are time itself.

Lure

The sea tilted toward me like a painting.
I could hang it from a hook in the sky.
No one about. A boat too far out
to see me. The water is high-tide-deep.
Unthinkable to plunge in. Unthinkable not to.

The Red Sofa

IX

For almost as long as the girl could remember, slipcovers in the form of an oatmealy synthetic fabric had been stretched over the old sofa, to conceal midnight-blue velvet upholstery which, as a child, she'd loved.

Her mother and father first bought the sofa on the occasion of their marriage in 1934, and it had travelled with them from their first, rather luxurious apartment in Manhattan, to this one in Queens, when their first child arrived.

The term 'shabby-chic' had not yet been coined. In any case, the mother would not have been sufficiently confident to follow that old-money style of English decorating, the one that gloried in revealing the worn-out velvet, the tired arm-rests, the threadbare patches where heads and bottoms had, over the years, made their marks.

Plans to upgrade this temporary measure were a constant subject of discussion, which heightened in intensity if guests were expected.

News

If it arrives with breakfast, you might
struggle to read the small print properly.
You might need a companion to decipher it
and to help you shoulder its impact.

Alternatively, it could be that you're
eavesdropping at an intimate gathering,
at lunch, for example, on Christmas Day,
and a word, or someone's name, floats idly
into the room, reaching you
as you stand, champagne flute in hand;
you're wearing your well-cut velvet jeans
and last year's ever so pointy-toe boots.

Have you assumed up to now that
when I said 'news' I'm referring only
to bad news? It could so easily be
otherwise. However. If news doesn't arrive
at the right time—too soon, before you're ready for it,
you might ignore it, toss it aside, however good.
Too late, and news deteriorates. Not unlike fresh fish—

at first so silvery, wet and clear-eyed, wrapped
in what we're talking about—yesterday's news.
So what's your news?
If it's old, it won't be fit for the cat to steal.

Two Chairs

If I were sitting in this chair, with you
alongside in this identical one,
both of us leaning slightly forward
facing the dancing fire as we talked,
knowing that the fire was also dancing
on the polished floorboards, that all of it—
two chairs, our backs, the fire—was reflected
in the shimmer of the living room mirror,
this winter evening might have been one
to recall, perhaps mention, years from now
in a memoir. As it is, both chairs are empty.
The mirror has blackened. You are lost;
I am busy dismantling the house: books,
walls, floor—all of it consumed by fire.

The Friend

In a circle of friends, the one who dies first
is the friend you will never forget:
this is the death that liberates you
from the trappings of everyday life
and makes you—suddenly—absurdly grateful
for each new breath—beginning with this one.

This is the death that persuades you to turn away
from whatever refuses to speak to your heart
from whatever threatens to numb your soul
from whatever it is that revels in death.

Keep the memory of this death as fresh
as the memory of your friendship.
Listen. Together they urge you: *Live your life.*

Late Flowering

The petalled, double D cups of our *magnolia*
soulangiana have given way to leaves
and the scent of lilac is a memory.
Thanks to pruning, the roses are in full bloom
creating a foil for the annual
August show of our fragile Japanese
anemones, massed and commanding in
their long-stemmedness, holding their own
into September, as the winds begin to bite
and the gusty rains shake the ripening
apples to the ground, where the waiting worms
will drill their holes. And now the Naked Ladies
make their appearance—pink and shameless
in their late flowering. I vow to follow suit.

Note:
'Naked Ladies' is the common term for *Amaryllis Belladonna:* three to
four pale pink, sweetly scented, trumpet-shaped flowers which appear on
bare stems in September and October.

The Red Sofa

X

None of the guests who came and sat ever suspected that this bland, slip-covered sofa was the centrepiece of so many family pow-wows, discussions which began with a simple notion to replace the sofa and ended with heady five-year plans for the economic restructuring, and possible relocation, of the family's entire life.

Nor could the guests have imagined the faded velvet grandeur that lay beneath that thrifty, slightly knobbly, decidedly unpleasant beige solution. But after they had left, the mother would invariably insist how very much better the evening would have gone had the sofa been more elegant.

The first thing the girl does is to restore the sofa to what she considers its former beauty with a silk-ribboned rose damask.

She runs her hand down its smooth back, recalling how, years ago, the raised stripes of velvet would print fine lines on her cheek as she dreamed through the long afternoons of her childhood.

The Returning Resident

Imagine there remained just the pair of you—
binoculars trained on your every move,
twitchers gathering in flocks year on year
to note whether you've reproduced your kind.

Reduced to an icon, or elevated,
depending on your point of view. Alive,
yet nowhere to be seen except on crests.
Sure, you have cousins who resemble you—

hook-billed or hooded, carrion-eating types,
reprobates with a penchant for stealing;
some solitary, others whose mad rookeries
ring with their raucous cries.

Yet you remain a rarity. Each Spring
out of grey-brown spotted eggs, pop feathered heads
in a crevice in a cliff, or deep inside
a cave, blacker than your wings, to shelter

your fledglings, still few enough to count
on the fingers of one hand. How long before
you reclaim your natural habitat?
Scarlet-billed, you'll soar above the thrift-strewn

coast, exploring every cleft, retrieving
insects for your young, lifting off the page
at last, as your particular kind of crow
with triumphant *chee-aws* comes into its own.

Open to the Weather

In this, our fifth winter,
storms lasso the house.
A distant sea wall
buckles. The trains falter.
Telephones die.

Our sand-rich beach blackens
with weed and rock from God
knows where, and the tide
rises . . . stealing summer land.
The world becomes water.

I dress carefully and walk
full face into a Force 9 . . . crossing

the first field; the second;
at the third stile my dog

refuses. We are wind-whipped and
sodden. Go back, he pleads,

his head cocked in the direction
of home. Let's go back. That night

the roar of the chimney-wind peaks
and I hear you mutter in your sleep:
I can't take it

anymore. I can't
take it anymore.

★ ★ ★

The morning will be bright. Silent. The sea
will resolve into its cat's eye green,

the storm debris mustachioed with cream.
That clay pot we placed in the shallow cleft

on the far terrace will not have shifted
an inch, as if it were the hollowed out

eye of the now-spent storm. Our dog will sleep
his morning sleep in the winter-thin

shadow of the granite balustrade
with the wind's shaping hand ruffling his dreams.

Tiepolo Blue

By morning, thick furls of cloud have rolled in
as if a series of breakers from a winter sea

had broken free, floated up and formed a grey
ceiling above me, inches off the horizon line

settling in like a headache that won't shift,
sifting the light, muffling birdsong.

Later, toward evening, a brush stroke of
the tenderest blue—the canvas has been

pierced clean through, inadvertently revealing
the truth of another sky beyond this one.

Is that the sky the ancients looked up to
or one so new it's still being created?

I swear that the window of Tiepolo blue
would be wet to the touch if only

I could touch it. Perhaps I've glimpsed a scene
still in rehearsal in a parallel universe—

an accidental parting of the curtain
by a careless stagehand. I'm tantalized

by this sliver of clarity and light.
The vision stays with me throughout the night.

The Red Sofa

XI

The years pass quickly, much more quickly than her childhood.

She moves across town to another apartment with the man she will marry. The pale rose damask has darkened in places, and, more like her mother than she would ever care to admit, she decides to make it like new again.

To return it, in fact, to velvet, but in a wine red.

The marriage is troubled and brief. When the sofa moves with her again to another apartment, with another man, she knows that her mother wonders and worries about many things to do with her daughter's way of life.

But her mother's main line of questioning is why she persists with that old-fashioned, over-stuffed sofa. Her mother has, by now, twice replaced that Scandinavian one. First, with a busy chintz. Next, a low-slung, white modular affair.

Her father, totally accepting of his wife's taste, is simply relieved that neither of these more recent sofas sports stark, wooden arms.

On a rare visit to his daughter in her latest Manhattan apartment during his wife's Scandinavian period, he had expressed the theory, while nestling into his former sofa, that Scandinavians must have a preference for uncomfortable things, and that perhaps their unremitting diet of cold winters hardened them to discomfort.

Suitcases

Let's pack now, put our weekend selves into
these smart suitcases—you in this one,
me in that—and head out toward the tip of the Island
where sea spray gave the glorious old Inn its name.

We've packed clothes to play in, to swim in,
as if we're still children, though I know
you were not one of those whose parents
brought them here. This place holds nothing for you.

When your mother speaks with her neighbour from Lvov
you leave the room. You cannot stand the repetition
of their talk of suitcases, of packing, of leaving
everything; of her struggles to bring you up in Brooklyn;

of how lucky you are. Of how she misses her husband.
You cannot stand feeling lucky, even as we walk
along this oceanic landscape, the salt wind
scouring our city selves, giving us respite before we pack.

Years later, I stand where the white-shingled Sea Spray stood.
I knew that a mysterious fire, one winter night, had demolished it,
yet to see for myself this stretch of beach, unbuilt, unpeopled . . .
Nothing, I know, compared to the emptiness of Lvov.

Month of Moons

Dance with me—you're a sliver of silver—
I'll wear you like an earring,
a comma of light.

You're magnetic—dance with me—
lend me your shimmering half.
Meet me at midnight.

You are about to become . . .
Dance with me, and to *hell* with your shape.
Can I hold you tight?

You're the tango spangling the sea—
let's celebrate the rites,
shape-shift with light.

The Red Sofa

XII

The girl, no longer a girl, again moves abroad. She takes only her favourite clothes and books.

And for many years, the sofa, still in red velvet, is lodged in a huge warehouse somewhere in New Jersey.

She lives in a succession of flats and houses, and sits on countless sofas, none of them her own. So many of them are faded, and even slightly torn, especially in the grandest rooms, and she wishes her mother could sit alongside her now to see how relaxing it might have been to cherish her unprepossessing sofa; to accept, even in the most superficial ways, the passing of time.

After five years, this transplanted daughter has all her things sent to her. Some things she had forgotten she owned.

And in a house which she imagines she has settled into, she installs the resplendent red sofa which she occasionally naps on, warmed by pale winter sunlight, the book she is reading slipping from her grasp as the sentences run together.

So Soon, So Soon
for Fred

One word at a time, I'll begin losing
what I know of the world, forgetting first
the name of a friend, or the cove we used to
walk toward; things you'll quickly fill in for me.

Then, linking a string of words will be beyond me.
Half-formed sentences will pile up like stalled cars
rusting beneath snow. As bright days dissolve into
purple afternoons, flurries will keep swirling upward
past the closed window, long into the night.

And when whole chapters have receded,
you'll recall them for me with a word—*seems like yesterday,*
I'll whisper. Here, on my pulse, I plan to write
your name. Mine's already on this tight white
bracelet, last name first—as if I could forget *that!*
Or where I am now, and so soon, so soon.

A Writer's Beach

An exultation of larks . . . murmuration
of starlings . . . *a garrulousness of gulls*?
As I follow the lip of froth, sea birds
by the dozen lift off, only to resettle
further down the beach, nestling in the sand
like warm-blooded stones: an artist's installation.
Amidst their screaming conviviality,
I note the feathers that mark their passage:

a long curving grey, a dainty white comma,
and this—a downy, chocolate brown—each find
a perfect quill. Clearly, what brings me here
isn't simply the white-lipped waves beneath
ink-splattered skies, but these birds, oceanic
birds on the wing—each lending me a pen.